The Intelligent Immigrant

How a genius person achieves
the life goal by immigration

A global guide with
real-life examples

Steve Hosseini

The Intelligent Immigrant

Address all inquiries to
info@smartmanagementcentre.com

ISBN Paperback: 9780646824604

Contents

Introduction 4

1. Why Immigration?. 9
The reasons for immigration and the logic
behind this decision

2. Before Moving 19
Preparation before immigration to guaranty
your future success

3. Baggage 37
What you should take with you

4. Arrival & Accommodation 41
Most accessible and economical options
after arrival

5. Settlement 44
How to settle in the best condition

6. Shocks 96
Language, culture, finance and other unexpected
challenges

7. Deep Dive 105
Job-hunting, business, and related challenges

8. Boost your growth 139
How to fully grow up and achieve your
critical goals

9. Final Word 144

Introduction

I had in mind for a while, the idea of writing this book. Finally, the Covid-19 lock-down provided the best opportunity for me as I stayed home for a couple of months, and this was the time I achieved my goal to write this important and unique book.

One day, the idea of this book came to my mind when I thought, I'm very successful as an immigrant. I have moved to Australia nine years ago and started from deficient positions in this country. Despite many different challenges, I achieved some worthwhile goals together with my lovely wife, and my two adorable kids.

I also saw so many people in this journey with success and failure. I'm not writing this book from gathering information, but I was really in the middle of the fire and touched all aspects of this journey with my body and mind.

I thought it would be valuable to share my experiences and discoveries from my journey and many other people's story with people around the world. People who want to take similar actions and similar pathways in their life, as I always like to help people in any matter than I can.

Of course, I have made so many smart moves together with many mistakes, and I'm sure that explaining both scenarios can help you on this journey.

I wrote this book a way that anyone with any level of education, profession, and nationality with any kind of visa be able to gain from my story. I mentioned my specific examples together with general solutions, and recommendations in this book, so that the solutions presented in this book are not specific for someone like only my profession, or only for people from my home country.

Now that I explained the points mentioned earlier, I will introduce myself.

I was born and grew up in Iran (Former known as Persia), studied Bachelor, and Master of Mechanical Engineering in Iran, and worked 14 years as Engineer, and Manager in four different industries in that country.

I worked as Production Engineer, Product Engineer, Factory Manager and Vice president, Project Manager, and Technical Deputy in the automotive industry, automotive parts manufacturing, and Electrical industries in Iran.

I moved to Australia nine years ago, at the age of 37 with my family having a skilled visa as an Engineer, and lived in Australia with my family until now.

Even though I traveled to many countries during my work in Iran, and I have contacted many different cultures. Still, I encountered a lot of challenges once I have immigrated permanently to Australia, and I think this is the case for many people.

The language challenge, the cultural shock, job hunting struggle, kid's settlement, financial hardship, emotional ups and downs, homesickness, and so on, are the minimum to mention.

Only if you move to a new country with the same language and a similar culture with the same level of development, you will have very minimal challenges which are not very common.

In this book, I tried to share my story and experiences with so many other people's accounts as useful examples of possible solutions to these challenges. I tried to introduce more solutions that are possible, even if I didn't use them, or I didn't know I could do them at the time. But, please be innovative and open-minded to expand the potential solutions for your new environment, and the new country.

For sure, I'm not able to cover everything, and I included many examples from so many different countries. I also mentioned some more detailed information about Australia, because I lived here. But none of them in concept is specific to Australia. I'm sure you can find similar or equivalent solutions in your new home.

Finally,
- If you never thought about immigration
- If you are not sure to immigrate or not
- If you have decided already to immigrate
- If you have applied or you are going to apply
- If you are on the journey today
- If you have moved already, but you want to achieve your life goals
- If you have moved already, but you are not happy

- If you have moved already, you are happy, but you didn't achieve your full potential yet

This book is for you. I hope you enjoy reading this book, and if you have any idea for improvement, please help me with emailing me to info@smartmanagementcentre.com

Steve Hosseini

Chapter 1

Why Immigration?

I included this chapter because this is the starting point of the journey, and many people even are not sure they should move or not. I will try to make this chapter as a guide of decision making for people who haven't decided yet to immigrate.

People immigrate for many different reasons, including but not limited to:
- Political pressure
- Economic struggle
- Family circumstances
- Social insecurity
- War
- Professional endeavor
- Improvement in living condition

- Freedom
- Kid's future goals
- Country corruption
- Etc.

Some people decide to move as a result of one of the scenarios mentioned above, but for some people, it's more than one reason, like myself, and my family. I immigrated because of the mixture of many reasons. Let me share my story with you.

We have an annual entrance exam called "Konkur" for universities in Iran, as the population of people wanting to study at university is almost ten times bigger than all universities' capacity.

My ranking was 461 in this exam, which means between 1.1 million participants, I was the number 461 top person as per my scores. I secured my study at the best Technology University in Iran called the "Sharif University of Technology."

I completed my Bachelor, and have been accepted for a Master's degree in Bu-Ali Sina University and completed my master's degree in due course.

I had a lot of big dreams, like establishing my business, starting my factory, and to get rich one day. The reason for having these ambitious goals was not that I loved money but because I came from a middle-class family and was passionate about doing big things, influencing people around me, my society and help the world.

But, despite having a bachelor, and master's degrees in one of the best majors from one of the best universities, I was not able to find a job with fair competition. Employers didn't give me any chance to prove myself.

Finally, one of my friends introduced me to an employer as this is the typical approach in Iran. I got a job from this connection, not from my pure talent and degrees.

I worked for 14 years in Iran and married, and my salary was almost high in the last eight years, but I was not able to buy even a small 70 square meter apartment unit for my family.

Most young people are buying home with getting help from their parents in this country. Many of them do not marry, and work many years as a single person to save money, and buy a minimum unit for themselves.

My second job also was created by a connection. My brother's friend introduced me to that employer. As I said, this is quite common in Iran. But I was not satisfied with my job. After six years of work as an Engineer, I was able to secure a managerial position as a "Factory Manager and Vice President," purely based on my talent, and my capabilities. This job was a huge turning point in my career, as I was only 29 years old.

I had all kinds of authority in this role except finance, and I left this company after a long four years because this company had a huge financial struggle. Owners were borrowing money from the banks for the company, but instead of spending money on the company's growth, they were buying lands for gaining capital growth.

The real estate market encountered a broad and long term downtime, and they stuck in massive debt for the company. Employees had eight months with no salary payment.

I moved to another company as a "Technical deputy and Vice president," and stayed there until we immigrated to Australia.

We moved because of the following reasons:
1- Religious culture and religious government
2- Financial hardship

3- Job insecurity

4- Air pollution

5- Social crime

6- Concern about the future of my kids in a society with easy access to all kind of drugs

7- Country corruption

One day, My wife and I were discussing our options for the future, and we thought it would be good if we apply for immigration to Australia, as we are not sure how will be the living condition a couple of years after that. We were very thoughtful, and maybe lucky that we applied because when our visa granted three years after that, the condition was ten times worse.

Now that I'm writing this book, the people's living condition is a hundred times worse than the time we were in Iran.

It was a tough decision for us to leave our home, our country, our family, our friends, our network, and naturally everything in Iran. One of the main reasons for being a difficult decision for us was the point that we were pioneers in our family. No one from my family and my wife's family has done this before us.

People who have close family member, or a close friend immigrated overseas are deciding about this move very quickly, because they have explicit knowledge and information.

One thing I was sure was that no one immigrated to a developed country from Iran, returned to Iran, and this was the main point that we relied on, and decided to give it a shot.

Now I can recommend you this:

If you are not happy about your life, mainly because your country is not the right place, and you can't change it, moving to the correct land is one of the best solutions. Immigrating at a younger age will make you more successful in the new country.

Don't confuse this idea with the concept of running away from problems. Yes, we should always face difficulties and resolve them. If everyone who feels unhappy, leaves their country, who will build a country's future?

My answer is this. You should evaluate your situation and your country's reality. For example, think about innocent people suffering in Afghanistan. Do you think any Afghani individual can improve the country for a level of the standard living condition? Do you think even a constructive national party can do this?

I'm not pessimistic, but I try to be realistic. Only if a global consensus and a global will power come to act, and change the condition of Afghanistan, then you will hope this country will develop after maybe 20 years. But, with current circumstances, no way.

You can apply this example to your country and see what is happening. If your state has the basic of democracy and development like environment for independent parties and free newspapers, you can hope to make some impact.

A- If some robust and constructive parties are developing your country, stay, and support the improvements.

B- If you think you are powerful enough and you can make a great political party with your connections, friends, and network, stay and do it.

C- Suppose you can sacrifice your life and change your country like *Nelson Mandela* for South Africa, stay and do it. *Nelson* sentenced to life imprisonment and finally remained in jail for 27 years until he achieved his goal.

Another example is *Mohammad Mossadegh*, the prime minister of Iran in 1951. He nationalized the oil of Iran while it was under UK control. But after that, *Mosaddegh* was imprisoned for three years, then put under house arrest until his death and was buried in his own home to prevent a political furor.

D- If you have a national goal, you are ready to die, you are prepared to sacrifice your family, and you have power and money to act, stay in your country and do something to change your country and people's life.

But, if you live in a corrupted country and your hands are tight, don't waste your life. Even the heroes a lot bigger than you who sacrificed their lives were not able to fix your country.

You won't miss your country if it's in a hell-like condition. You will make new friends and a new network. You can make your new life much better than the one you have now.

If you have a concern about leaving your parents behind, you have one of these two scenarios:

Either you have a nuclear family or an extended family.

If you have a nuclear family, educate them about your possible future. Then move and make your new life ready for your parents to come after you. If you belong to an extended family, your siblings will take care of your parents if they don't like to move with you.

Some people think they should stay with their parents if they are not happy with them to move. Listen, if your parents are not thinking logically, and their lack of knowledge, their favor and selfishness will ruin your life and your kid's life, don't listen to them and do what is correct, and the best for you.

If you are religious, and you think you should stay in your corrupted country, because God wanted for you, and you will go to heaven after you die, I give you the following recommendations:

- Think out of the box
- Be skeptical
- Rely on science which is the only truth
- Judge with your brain

I tell you my findings which is not only mine, but there is much scientific evidence behind this truth:
No one can bring, and no one brought so far, even one little evidence for the existence of life after death and the presence of Hell and Heaven. No one can prove that also we have a soul.

So, why are you keeping all of your eggs in a broken basket? Why are you ruining your life by relying on something without any proof or evidence?

Please be realistic, and live your life. Make it better for yourself and your family. Support your siblings, and your parents if you can. Don't waste your life.

Think also about this scenario, if you leave your home country and it suddenly becomes like heaven after you left, you can come back any time you like with higher skills, knowledge, experiences, educations, and money.

So, think more than once, and put aside emotion when you decide about moving or not moving.

Chapter 2
Before Moving

A- Visa process

In this chapter, I will explain in summary the requirements of visa applications. Considering the point that each country has its process detail, I will mention only critical information, but I will also explain other vital elements before you travel.

1- How to apply

You can apply for a visa in two options:
- You apply yourself
- You pay a consultant or a lawyer to apply for you

Applying yourself is a low cost for you, but for many people, it is risky as they don't know all the rules, and they may provide incomplete evidence and documents, and the embassy rejects their application.

The second option is less risky, but it will cost you more.

I used the second option and paid one of the immigration companies to do it for me, and I was thrilled with the results and quick actions from them.

If you have a busy life, and you are not very good at reading particular governmental documents, I recommend you to get help. It's only about fifteen percent more cost.

I paid all together about 8000 USD for a family of four, including the embassy cost, and the consultant fee. If you have lots of time, and you are very good at computers and documents, and you want to save money, do it yourself.

Be careful, not to lie, and not to provide miss-leading documents. If they reject your application because of a low score, you can apply again later, but if they find you are not honest, you will go to black-list.

2- Skilled visa

If you have a skill or degree, you can apply for a skilled visa. For example:
- Doctor

- Engineer
- Nurse
- Teacher
- Carpenter
- Accountant
- Plumber
- Electrician
- Etc.

The countries of destination usually revise their skill demand list frequently, which directly affects your ability to get a visa or not. They alter their demand list based on the population of each skill and market status for those professions in the target country.

Each country has different requirements. For example, the embassy may ask you to provide mainly the following evidence and documents:
- Police check
- ID
- The evidence of your skills or degrees
- IELTS (International English Language Testing System) certificate
- Evidence of three years of professional work experience

- CDR, including a unique format with three professional projects
- Fee
- Etc.

ID stands for "Identity document." It's any pictured document that shows your identity like your passport or national ID card.

CDR and three projects are the professional packages that are showing you have done professional works, and you know what you are claiming.

The embassy gives you a score based on your documents and your experiences, which determines your eligibility for that visa. If you have a family member in that country, it will be a higher score for you.

Your family member from the target country can sponsor your application, and you will get more scores, and get your visa much more manageable.

If you received a skilled visa, it might be unlimited, which in this case, you can live in any city or area. But, recently, they grant only regional visas, which means you have to stay in a specific territory or state for a couple of years. Other than that, you won't have any limitations.

The process for your visa application will take a couple of years depends on your condition and the country of destination.

I got my visa almost two years after I submitted all of the required documents. A friend of mine applied for Canada, and his application took seven years as he changed his condition a couple of times during the process, including marriage, and adding his child to his visa application. One thing they check also is your history of crime and police check, including your name check for international crime.

The visa usually will be for five years, and it will be renewed automatically after that. In reasonable conditions, you can apply for citizenship after 4 to 5 years.

3- Business visa

If you are going to immigrate with a business visa, also each country has its different rules. The embassy will ask you mainly to provide:
- ID
- Police check
- Your business history and evidence
- Your finance history and evidence

- A lump sum money deposit, for example, $500K or more
- Etc.

Usually, you will receive a conditional visa, and you need to start a business and show profitability by two years. If you have business experience and supportive capital, this is a pretty easy way to immigrate.

But, after getting a visa and traveling over, you need to do actual work. Some people who have good capital, buy a business in their home country and claim as they are a business person. They also can buy a ready business like a pizza shop in the target country and manage it to the profitable status for finalizing their permanent visa and citizenship.

4- Student visa

If you are going to apply for a student visa, you will need to provide at least the following documents:
- ID
- Usually two recommendations from your professors
- Detail of your degree and scores
- Financial support
- Etc.

Usually, a student visa is together with limited working permission, which is good to make some money during the study.

You need to search thoroughly, and clarify for yourself the following points:

- Which country do you want to go?
- Which university do you prefer to study?
- Which major do you like to study, and what degree?
- What is the market condition for that specialty you want to study?
- What's you plan after completing your degree? You want to stay in that country, or you want to move to another place, or you want to come back?
- What's the cost per term and year?
- What's your plan to cover the cost?
- Can you secure a scholarship for your study at that university?
- Are you allowed to work during the study to help with your cost?
- Do you have any friends there?

All of these questions can help you to make an intelligent decision, and these are the first stones of building your future. You don't want to ruin your life. The right choice and a good degree in a developed country worth a fortune.

So, think, and search thoroughly, and choose the best options for your future.

5- Refuge visa

If you are going to immigrate as a refuge, the condition is not very clear and constant. Some people are coming by boat illegally. I don't recommend this as many of them are dying with their family in the ocean.

Some people apply through the embassy before they travel, which is a safer way. You should provide genuine evidence and reasons for your refugee application, for example, government threat, or other issues, to be able to receive this type of visa.

If they accept you as a refugee, the government provides many different social and economic supports to you. Consider the point that, if you granted a refuge visa as a result of your condition with political reasoning, highly likely, you wouldn't be able to visit your home country in your life-time, unless that government changes.

I met many people who came with refuge visas and started their own business as a mechanic, carpenter, or excavator.

It's your life, and if you have a better choice, don't choose a refuge visa.

B- After granting visa

You need to consider the following topics, after receiving your visa:

1- Documents

Make sure you collect all the necessary materials like:

- ID
- Passport
- Certificates
- University degrees
- Kid's immunization history
- Etc.

You need to translate them to be able to use them in the destination country. Usually, translation cost in your country is lower than a developed country.

An international driver's license will be useful in some countries. In some cases like Australia, you can drive with your original translated driver's license for six months.

2- Skills

You need to research the country of your destination to understand what skills or certificates are useful to achieve. If you don't have any skills, go and learn something. For example:

- Hairdressing
- Tailoring
- Tiling
- Carpentry
- Child Care certificate
- Taxi Driving
- Gardening
- Landscaping
- Plumbing
- Electrician
- Etc.

If you have a professional degree and experience, find out what is famous for your profession. For example, I learned the Inventor and Solidworks, which are useful for Mechanical Engineering.

3- Language

Try to learn the language of that country before you fly to it. Starting life without knowing the language of the new home will be a disaster. For English, you can do as below:

- IELTS classes

- Watching and listening to ABC channels
- Watching BBC and CNN channels
- Watching original language movies
- Traveling overseas
- Etc.

What did I do? I completed my IELTS certificate. Then I asked one of my colleagues, a foreign commercial staff, to speak with me only in English. Farsi forbidden.

If your visa didn't need the language competency, spend some time to learn the minimum of required language skills to be able to communicate during your travel. This minimum skill will save you a lot of time and makes your travel stress-free.

For the minimum, you can write down the main sentences, which you predict you will need in your travel, and keep it with yourself just in case you are stuck, and you have to communicate.

In my case, I needed an overall score of six for the IELTS certificate and a minimum of six for each skill of "Speaking, Reading, Listening and Writing," and I received a higher score. Also, I paid almost 3000 USD for my wife as she didn't have an IELTS certificate. With this payment, we secured a free English class for a couple of months in Australia after we arrived in a governmental organization called "AMES."

4- Money

Once you arrived, you don't know how long you will be unemployed and have to spend from your savings. If you want to reduce your stress and secure your stay, you need to have adequate savings.

You can transfer money to a friend's account overseas before you fly, or take cash with you, and deposit it in your new account once you arrived.

The best option is as follow:
- Google and find any bank in the target city
- Or ask a friend in target city to introduce you the best bank
- Contact the bank by phone or email
- Send the certified copy of your ID to bank
- Open a bank account

- Transfer your money to your bank account
- In case you canceled your immigration, you can transfer back your money by their internet banking

A certified copy is a copy of a document in which you ask an authority to sign and seal it. The administration can be a Police station, Pharmacist, or a Court.

Warning:

Information, as mentioned above, is correct for most of the banks in the developed countries. But, each bank has a different approach. Check with the bank about all the above possibilities, including opening accounts, transferring money to and from your account while you are still in your home country. Don't risk your money.

If it's not possible to open an account, you have to take some cash with you on your flight, then ask someone to transfer the remaining of your money to your new bank account after your arrival.

Prepare a plan with one of your close family member, or a close friend to be able to convert your assets to cash, and send it to you when needed.

5- Plan B

Let say you moved to a new country, and because of any reason, you were not successful. For example, you spent all of your savings, and you were not able to find a job. What is your plan B? Do you have a backup plan? Backup money or career to return?

Having a backup plan is an ideal situation which some people consider for themselves, and I saw some people- let say very few people- returned to their home country. For example, a bank manager from Sri Lanka, he was not able to find a proper job in Australia and returned to Sri Lanka after only six months. A friend of mine, a Mechanical Engineer, returned to Iran after only six months, as he was not able to get a job in Australia too.

But, be careful, this topic is very controversial. If this Bank manager or that Mechanical Engineer didn't have plan B of returning home, they would tolerate more than short six months, and they would do casual jobs until they find a better job. So, they could stay in Australia after coping with challenges, and now they had a better life in Australia.

So, having a plan B of returning is not always helpful. I think I stayed and copped with enormous challenges and hardship in the first year in Australia because I didn't have this plan B. If I had any chance to return home, staying in my home country until now was a disaster.

So, be thoughtful. I think the best way is to secure your stay in the destination country for a longer time without income or be ready to do any job to survive until achieving your goals. In another way, I agree with the mind-set that saying "if you decided to move, and you are sure your home country is not the place to be, it's better to burn all bridges behind you." In this way, you don't have any chance to return, and this will guaranty your successful stay and future.

The good news is that these days at least you can do ride-sharing driver jobs like Uber and

DiDi and survive. These options didn't exist back nine years ago when I was struggling with my cost of living.

6- Emotional roller coaster

Once you receive your visa, you will feel happy and sad at the same time if your situation is similar to mine. It's a mixed emotion as you are so glad to achieve your goal, and at the same time, you will miss your family. My sister was crying when I visited her for the last time. I told her, don't cry, we will see each other again.

But you know, at the end of the day, you are leaving them forever. You will visit them once every two or five years, but they will not see you often.

And, sometimes you won't be able to see them for a long time. What can we do, any action in life has pros and cons. We should evaluate our activities and do them when there is a huge benefit.

7- Destination city

Before you buy tickets, you need to search and find out which city is a better place for you and your family. Some criteria are as below:

- Population

- Job availability
- School quality
- Local language and accent
- Cost of living
- Beauty of city
- Available entertainments
- Climate
- Culture
- People's attitude toward immigrants
- Having a family member or friend
- Etc.

I have chosen Melbourne because of the following reasons:
- Job availability
- Having a friend
- Lower cost of living compare to Sydney

You can gather information through:
- Google search
- Talking to people and friends overseas
- Asking airline personnel
- Asking immigration consultants or your lawyer

8- Temporary accommodation

If you have an international credit or debit card like a master card or visa card, you can search for accommodation in the target city, and book accommodation online. I recommend you to book for two weeks initially.

If you don't have a credit card, but you have a friend overseas, you can ask your friend to find and book your temporary accommodation. You can search on google, and find some accommodations, and ask the taxi driver to take you to those addresses once you arrived. In the worst-case scenario, you still won't have a problem. You can request a taxi driver to help you with finding a hotel, motel, or inn, which is not an intelligent approach.

In some airports, also hotels have small offices, and staff for arriving people to book accommodations for them.

Chapter 3
Baggage

There are two options you can do:
1- Sell everything and fly
2- Ask a family member to freight your stuff after you arrived

We did the first option. We sold everything and lived in my mother-in-law's house for three weeks until we fly. In this way, you have the luxury of making your stuff new in your new place.

A couple of friends of mine, shipped their stuff after they arrived. In this way, some people feel happier as they have their stuff, and will not miss their home.

In option 1, you need to keep following stuff with you in your baggage:
- Your documents
- Money
- ID

- Medications
- Certificates and degrees
- Simple foods and snacks, especially if you have young kids

In option2, you will have less stress, as you need to carry only some necessary stuff, but it is more costly for you.

Photo albums are the useful stuff that you need to consider, as they will refresh your memories and gives you better feelings once you feel a little home-sick. Ask someone to send them to you after your travel if they are bulky. But, honestly, we never felt home-sick, neither my wife nor my kids.

Some people, especially singles, will feel a little lonely, and miss home and family. But, if they make friends, and expand their friend's network, they will feel better.

Make sure you check with your airline about the weight limit of your baggage, and carry-in bags according to your tickets.
Following caution points are very serious:

- Do not put cash and expensive stuff in your baggage- Thieves will steal them from your luggage. Keep your money in your pocket, or your handbag inside the cabin with you

- Wrap your baggage with plastic wrap which is available in many airports
- Wrap all brittle items with thick clothes if you have to put them in your baggage

Never put money in the luggage. A thief stole all cash that my Managing director had placed in his baggage without telling us on one of our overseas travels. If you wrap your baggage, first of all, it will protect your luggage against harsh handling, which is common, and secondly, thieves have less chance to open it and re-wrap it to steal your stuff. Unfortunately, this sort of problem is real, and you cannot avoid them.

Make sure you arrive at the airport two to three hours before your flight time. If you live far from the airport, travel to the city of the airport at least one day before your flight. We had a severe car accident the day before our flight while moving from my hometown to the capital city, which we had our trip.

Minimize all risks and stresses as much as possible. I was taking all of my savings in cash with me, which was very stressful. If you can, transfer it before or after your travel to your account.

Some countries like Dubai fine you for some medications like codeine. Some country like Australia has strict rules for stuff you bring into the country. For example, some dry foods, herbs, animals, etc., are prohibited. Don't be foolish to take illegal stuff, and make trouble for yourself and your family.

For incoming to some countries, you need to fill a two-page-form in the plane, which is your detail, and your target address, and the stuff that you have with you. Cash delivery also has limitations for some countries, and you can check with your airline about it.

Chapter 4
Arrival and Accommodation

1- Transport

If you are three or four people or more with baggage, you need two taxis or take a van. We call the van taxi, the "Maxi." In some cities, you can use Metro or Bus, which is more economical. These days as you are probably aware, there are cheaper options like rideshare services, including:

- Uber
- DiDi
- Ola
- Etc.

If it's possible, you can ask a friend to pick you up from the airport. I saw this with many people. They do this to help and make a good feeling for new arrivals.

2- Temporary stay

You have the following options once you arrive, which depends on your circumstances:

- Stay in your friend's home for a short time like a couple of days, and book accommodation for two weeks after that, then rent a house
- Stay in your friend's home until you rent a house
- Stay in a housing, which you booked before your flight, and search for a renting house
- Stay in accommodation for two to three weeks, and seek to buy a house

For a temporary stay, you have the following options:

- Student accommodation
- Shared unit
- Furnished unit or apartment
- Airbnb
- Apartment hotel
- Inn
- Motel
- Hotel

I put cheaper options on the top of the list.

Be open-minded, and search for the best and most economical options.

I know someone with a PhD degree, and two kids stayed in a student accommodation center for a couple of months and rented a house after he found a job.

We stayed the first two nights at my friend's house, then booked an apartment for two weeks. After that, I rented a unit before ending two weeks.

Singles usually use shared house. They rent one room from a home. Students typically use student accommodations, which is very economical.

Airbnb is people's home, which they put for rent. It can be a full house or a single room from a house.

Chapter 5
Settlement

In this chapter, first of all, I will give you some insight into priorities. Then, I will explain so many useful matters which I learned after many years of living in a developed country, and you can't find this information anywhere, unless you live year by year, and find out slowly.

1- Rent a property

Renting is a challenge for some people, as some of the real estates and landlords won't give their property to you when they noticed you don't have a job. I didn't have this problem when I showed my bank savings, but a friend of mine had a real struggle.

The best solutions for this problem are:
- Paying three to six months of rent in advance

- Providing your saving details from your bank account
- Providing evidence of government support if you have any- In Australia, Centrelink pays a family benefit to you if you have kids, and you don't have a job. They will also pay a little support for rent

The government pays better money to jobless people after two years stay in the country as a "New start" payment. Refugees get support immediately from the first day of granting asylum.

For renting, or buying a place for living, you have the following options- Lower expense on the top:
- Apartment
- Unit
- Townhouse
- House

When you search for renting a property, consider the following points:
- Find out the leading real estate websites of that country- Like " realestate.com" in Australia.

- Search in the website for suitable properties, and list down the inspection time, and the address.
- Ask a friend to help you with his car for your inspections, if possible.
- Inspect as many properties as possible before signing a contract.
- Fill application for any item which looks suitable for you- Filling a form is not a commitment.
- Have detail of two friends handy as some real estates need local referees for your application.
- Offer three to six months advance payment if you can afford in your application when you don't have a job.
- Consider a one-month advance payment of rent and another equivalent of one month rent as a Bond, which is usually required. Landlord and real estate will keep bond until you evacuate the house without damage. They will use bond money to repair the home after you damaged the property if needed.
- Reduce your expectation because you don't have a job yet.

Real estate and the landlord will review the applications and choose the best candidate. Then they call you and invite you to sign a contract. After signing the contract, and giving you the key, you will receive a "Condition report," which is a document showing the latest status of the property in detail.

You must review the condition report in detail room by room, and match with the real condition of the property. If real estate missed mentioning any damage in the condition report, you need to add to the document and return it to the real estate.

Make sure you keep a copy of the story. This document will help you to avoid any extra cost of repair for the time you evacuating the property at the end of the contract period.

When you are inspecting properties to find a suitable property, consider the following options as the positive points:

- Being close to a shopping center
- Being close to the park
- Being close to public transport
- Being close to school
- Having a wide driveway
- Having a proper cooling and heating system

- Not being very old
- Having a beautiful view, landscape, and back yard
- House has better independence than the unit

Too close to the metro is not a good option, because of the sound of the trains.

Usually, real estate runs regular inspections, mostly every six months, to make sure you keep their property in good condition. At the end of your rental contract, you have to do the following preparations after the evacuation, and before delivering the key to real estate:
- Complete cleaning by yourself or by a professional cleaning company
- Professional carpet cleaning
- Repair all damages you made

After you delivered the key, real estate will do a final inspection, and if you damaged anything, they would use your bond to repair the damages.

2- Buy a property

If you have good capital to buy a property in addition to money to cover your living cost for maybe one to two years, buying a property is an excellent idea because:

- You will settle permanently, and feeling better
- You will gain capital growth as a result of property appreciation

Again, the specific sites for the real estate market are the best place to search. It's better to do your homework and find out which area or suburb has good accessibility and excellent potential for appreciation.

The price will vary a lot depends on the city and area. For example, in a town, you can buy a house from a couple of hundred thousand dollars to a couple of million dollars.

If you need a loan to buy a property, you must have a job, and provide at least three months of payslip. Usually, you must have in your saving a minimum of eight to ten percent of the total property value to be able to secure a home loan.

When you buy a property, it's better to get support from a broker for your home loan. A good broker can find the best deals of investments with the lowest interest for you without any charge because they get their commissions from the bank. In some cases, you also need a conveyancer to settle legal documents for you.

One important thing to consider in countries with a high inflation rate is that their currencies are depreciating every day comparing to, for example, USD or AUD. So, if you have a property in your home country, it's an excellent idea to sell it and make it as a deposit to buy a property in your new country, which usually will be a developed country.

In many cases, real estate runs an Auction to sell their property to the highest offer from all buyers. You should observe a couple of Auctions before actively participate in the Auction process as a real buyer.

You have another option to become a homeowner. You can buy land and contract a builder to build your house. This way is useful if you would like to make as per your floor plan.

Another option is pre-purchasing a land under development. You can pay ten percent deposit, and secure an under development land.

One to two years after that, the land is ready, and you can build your house. Sometimes, you will gain a good appreciation for the price of the property, because the developer company pre-sells the land with a price lower than the market price for a ready-to-build area.

3- Government stuff

If you have some cash with you, opening a bank account, and depositing your money will be your priority. Ask your friends which bank gives you higher interest, and which one has got a better service.

Then ask these questions, and find out from anyone possible:
- What is the Public transport website or app?
  Like "PTV" in Victoria, Australia.
- What is the government site for medical support?
  Like "Medicare" in Australia.
- What is the central government office for immigration?
  Like "Ceterlink" in Australia.
- What is the tax office website?
  Like "ATO" in Australia.

The next step is to register for the departments mentioned above. You may go personally to their office, or register online. The tax office will dedicate a tax file number "TFN" for each adult.

4- Shopping

As you may know, each country or city has particular brands, individual stores, and specific areas for selling different products. When you want to buy anything in a new country, first of all, ask people around you for specialized markets.

For example, you can search for the following deals:
- Which store is selling the best-priced foods and groceries?
  Like "Aldi," "Coles," and "Woolworth" in Australia.
- Which store is selling the best-priced furniture?
  Like "Super Amart," "Harvey Norman," and "Fantastic Furniture, in Australia
- Which store is selling the best-priced stationery?
  Like "Officeworks" in Australia.
- Which store is selling the best priced electronic stuff?

Like "JB HiFi," and "Jaycar," in Australia

If you have limited savings, you can buy second-hand stuff like furniture and TV, etc. Ask for second-hand stores like "Salvos" and "Op Shop" or others in your country.

If you have a job, you can use finance to purchase anything, including furniture, TV, car, computer, Xbox, etc., and pay by installment, for example, through four years instead of paying in advance. Some stores offer interest-free finance as well.

There are some shops which are importing goods from China, and selling at little prices like "Two dollar shop," or "Reject shop."

If you are a strict Muslim, you can buy Halal meat from Muslim shops.

In some areas of some capital cities, the price of goods and groceries is lower depends on the average income of the population in that specific area.

When you shop in big supermarkets, you can borrow a trolley by inserting one or two dollars coin to the cart, and you will get your money back once you returned the trolley to the trolley station. You can also buy a trolley token, and use it as a coin.

You also can receive cash from your bank card while you are paying for your purchase in most of the big shops and supermarkets. We call it "Cash out."

5- School

Enrolling your kids in school usually is very easy. You can just search in google for "primary, or high school near me," and visit a couple of them. Then choose the one with a better environment, and better management, and staff.

You may want to enroll your kids in the best school in the area. In this case, you need to search and do your homework to find out the best-ranked school. You can google for ranking of school in your city.

If your child doesn't know the language, there will be some "language school" in some countries.

A young kid may need to stay in the language school a couple of months, or two terms to be able to learn minimum language skills, then you will transfer them to a mainstream school, and they will grow their language over there.

Child care and kinder garden are also straightforward to enroll. Some governments provide a level of support called "child care rebate," and this can help you with the cost. The government usually provides this support if one parent is studying, for example, is learning the language.

In general, don't concern about the language level of your kids. Usually, kids can learn a new language in a couple of months. My four-year-old son started the kinder garden without knowing even one English word. He began to say long English sentences in less than three months.

Public schools in some countries like Australia are free, but they ask you for voluntary support payments and some special payments, for example for camping. But, of course, the fee is mandatory in some other countries.

Camping is one of the best opportunities to improve your child's social skills and independence, but it's not mandatory.

If you would like to enroll your kids in a private school, make sure you choose the appropriate one for you as some of them are religious, and if you don't want your child to be spiritual or you have a different religion, they won't suit your child. Please consider the cost as well, which is a couple of thousand dollars per year or more.

Schools usually invite parents for a regular parent-teacher-student interview, which is a perfect time to review your child's progress in the school.

In developed countries, schools teach students by practical, teamwork-based, and experimental approaches instead of simple theory-based methods, which are the case in many old fashion countries.

During the years, they have some special events, and special days like pajama day, which is a free dressing day for all students.

6- University

If you or your child need to enroll in a university, you need to search and contact them and find out the best university for you. If you are a permanent resident or citizen, in some countries, you can use the governmental loans for university fees, and pay it back after getting a job, and making income. If your income is lower than a threshold, the government will postpone your repayment. We call this loan the "Fee-Help."

You can study for lower degrees like Diploma or Certificates in other organizations like:
- "Tafe"- Technical and Further Education
- RTO- Registered Training Organization

Generally speaking, you have so many options to study and improve your ability to secure a job in these countries. You may find some courses free for you depends on your visa status as governments want to support new arrivals.

7- Buy a car

I bought a car after five months stay, which was not the right decision. A friend told me it's better to buy a car once I got a job. You need a car from the first month of arrival to do your daily activities, shopping, kid's school, etc.

You also need a car to go to the interviews. Besides, you can do some casual jobs with your car.

To buy a car, usually, there are some specialized websites in each country. Search, and find out.

In Australia, the best are "carsales.com.au" and "gumtree.com.au."
Be careful to use local websites, not international ones, for this purpose of being safe from scams.

For example, most of the Australian company's website has the ".com.au" at the end of their web address.

You have two options to buy a car:
- Buy a new or used car from a dealership
- Buy a used car from a private owner

In the case of the dealership, usually, the price is higher. If you are buying a brand new car, a dealership will be the best option because of the warranty and services.

In the case of the used car, dealers usually won't provide a warranty, and you will be alone in case of car failure. I never recommend dealers for a used car. I bought a Ford used car for $5200. Every aspect of the vehicle was perfect for one month. Just after one month, all sides of the engine started leaking oil. I couldn't figure out how the dealer was able to hide this issue from my sight. After only two years, when I bought a brand new car, I was not able to sell my old car for more than $2000. Yes, I lost $3200.

Of course, some of them are fair too.

In all cases, you can call the seller and arrange an appointment for inspection. Ask a friend for his help with his car to drive you to the inspection address; otherwise, you have to go with public transport or taxi.

After inspecting a couple of cars, and choosing the good one, find a mechanic to come with you for the final inspection. A mechanic can assure you the car has no engine issue or other main problems. Then you can sign the form and pay a deposit. The mechanic may charge you $200.

You also can ask the insurance companies like "RACV" in Australia to do the technical inspection for you. They will charge you a little higher than a mechanic.

In Australia, the seller should provide a certificate of Roadworthy, which is a formal inspection by accredited centers shows the car is safe to drive.

Don't skip your mechanic inspection even if the seller provides a Roadworthy certificate because this certificate is only about safety in the road, and they don't care about the health of the car.

After providing the certificate, you pay the full amount and take the car. Then you need to take the signed form to related authority, for example, "VicRoads" in Australia, to register the vehicle on your name with paying a fee.

Before buying a car, make sure your driver's license is valid for driving. If you are purchasing a vehicle in a large city like Melbourne, make sure you have a navigator either in your smartphone or as a standalone unit.

A friend of mine, actually a machinery designer, bought a car and drove home. He didn't expect to have trouble to reach his home in Melbourne without a GPS.

You can't believe this. It took my friend seven hours to reach home without a GPS in Melbourne instead of half an hour's drive. He achieved this success with the help of a friend, guiding him through his phone from home. Very funny.

8- Driver's license

In some counties, you can use an international driver's license. In other countries like Australia, you can drive six months by your standard driver's license issued in your country but translated.

But you have to take some driving sessions with an instructor to learn the rules, and roads then attend a test to get a country's valid driver's license.

I will explain the process in Australia as an example:
In Australia, the driver's license has three steps test as below. For other counties, you need to find out.

- Learner test- A multi-selection written test about the rules of driving
- Hazard test- A computer simulation test to evaluate your understanding about driving, and road hazard
- Final driving test- A forty-five minutes actual driving test in the road

You don't have to do all three tests in one run, but without completing these steps, you are not allowed to drive.

If you don't have experience of driving at all like a teenager, after Learner test, they will issue a Learner permit card, and post it to you. Then you have to drive 120 hours with the supervision of a full-license person and fill the log-book accordingly. Only after that, you can attend the hazard test and final driving test.

In this case, if you pass all tests, you will get a license as a red "P," and you must display the red "P" label both in front and back of your car for one year. After that, if everything goes fine, you will be issued a green "p" license for the next three years with displaying the green "P" label on your car. Only after that, will you become a full license. This process looks a little lengthy and complicated, but it's the best and safest approach which the government designed and implemented to reduce car accidents and mad driving.

A critical point is "Demerit Point." In some countries, you will receive one to three or more demerit points for each fault and penalty in your driving period. When you got twelve demerit points, Police authority will suspend your license for at least three months. Depends on the situation, you can release your license after that. Police will erase any demerit point after one year from the issuing date.

So, consider that, for a fault like passing a red light by mistake or deliberately, not only you pay the penalty like $400, you also lose three points.

9- Driving

For driving in developed countries, you must follow the rules. The penalties are stringent and painful.

I remember 20 years ago in Iran. I asked a European business manager who was working and living in Iran about his driving experience in Tehran. I expected to hear that driving is severe for him because people are not following the rules. Surprisingly, he said, the driving here is effortless. You don't need to follow any law. Just press the accelerator pedal, and go ahead.

But, here in developed countries, you have to follow all the rules, and very soon, you learn everything, and you feel that it's straightforward and relaxed driving: no stress and pressure.

10-   Roadside assistant

Back in Iran, we never had a roadside assistant. Whenever our car failed, we would catch a taxi, and find a mechanic shop, and ask them to come with us, and fix our car. Here in developed countries, this is not easy and economical. The best solution is registering for a suitable road-side assistant company like "RACV" in Australia. It's only a couple of hundred dollars per year, and you have peace of mind that anywhere in the country, someone will come and help you to fix your car, or to tow your vehicle to a mechanic shop.

Actually, without this service, I feel unsafe to travel because in many places, especially far from cities, you will be stuck alone. There is only a small weakness with the road-side assistant and its lack of mobile network in some areas.

11-   Job hunting

I explained a full story and solutions about this topic in chapter seven.

12-   Food and restaurants

There are many different fast foods and restaurants in every city in the world. For example, we have the following food services:

- Mac Donald's
- Hungry Jacks
- Red Roaster
- Nando's
- KFC
- Italian restaurant
- Persian restaurant
- Greek restaurant
- Thai restaurant
- Indian restaurant
- Steak house
- Etc.

Many of them have a "Drive-through" service, which you order, pay, and receive your foods without coming off your car. We also have many different supermarkets as I mentioned some of them already plus many specialized supermarkets like:

- Persian supermarkets
- Indian supermarkets
- Afghani supermarkets
- Thai supermarkets
- Etc.

So, as you can guess, you won't struggle with food. You can start with fast food while you are in a temporary stay, or even like us you can shop raw materials, and cook even in the motel or hotel. Only, some kids who are very fussy about food will have a problem, but still, you can find something for them to eat.

There are many bars you can go to and drink, or you can shop from supermarkets, and drink at home. The popular one in Australia is "Dan Murphy," and some supermarkets like Woolworth and Coles have their exclusive liquor shop next to them.

Selling Alcohol to under 18-year-old is prohibited in some countries. Drinking in the street or even delivering an open bottle in the road will result in penalty too.

13-   Entertainment and attractions

It's straightforward to search for entertainment or attractions of your city on Google, and you will find many places. Make sure you keep yourself healthy and fresh-minded while you are staying at home, maybe for a long time, and searching for your proper job. Visiting lovely places can boost your energy.

Some places to mention for Australia are as below:
- Melbourne zoo
- Melbourne aquarium
- Healesville sanctuary

- Fun field
- Luna park
- Philip Island
- Great ocean road
- Sovereign hill
- Gold coast and its theme parks
- Great barrier reef
- Blue mountain
- Opera house
- Cardinia Reservoir park
- Jells park
- Ruffy lake park
- Werribee zoo
- Gumbaya park
- Adventure park
- Cairns
- Melbourne museum
- Etc.

The list will go on and on.

For leisure activities, you will have many options depends on the city and country that you live. Some example for Australia are as below:

- Skiing
- Jetski
- Scuba diving

- Fishing
- Sailing
- Cycling
- Running
- Camping
- Kayaking
- Racing car
- Swimming
- Parachute
- Glider riding and piloting
- Hot air balloon riding
- Hiking
- Sports
- Making BBQ in the park
- Hiring Caravan and travel around
- Etc.

The list will go on and on.

14-   Toll

Mainly in large cities, you have to pay a toll for using the highways. In many countries, they have an electronic version of the toll payment. You buy a tag and attach it inside the front shield of your car, and the toll equipment installed in the highways will read it. The money will be deducted from your bank account as you set it before.

In some cases, you can buy one time pass ticket instead of buying a tag. But, if you don't pay toll in direct debit or inside the time window after using a highway, you will receive a penalty that is much higher than the original toll payment.

Some people think they are smart, and they don't use highways. They drive long ways to reach their destination, and most will pay more petrol costs than toll and take more time for them.

At the end of the day, as I experienced, using tollways is more economical than not using it.

15-   Ambulance

Once you arrived, check and find out the best option to register an ambulance service, as the ambulance is a very critical need for anyone. You can register with annual payment in some countries, for example, with only $120, or you can buy private medical insurance, including ambulance service. Either option, don't take risks with your emergency needs and make sure you register one.

16-   Emergency numbers

First thing you do in any country you want to live, ask for the following emergency numbers:
- Police
- Ambulance
- Fire Engine

In Australia, for example, all three numbers are triple zero,"000", and this will be your very critical information. Make sure your kids also learn and memorize these numbers.

17-   Fire

Find out which place near your property is the safest in case of fire. Teach your kids to evacuate the home, and run to that place in case of fire. Sometimes, the mail-box can be this safe place for them, but in some cases, you need to find a better place, maybe more distance from the fire.

Check your smoke detectors regularly, for example, once a month to make sure they are working. If their battery is flat, replace them, and if they are faulty, report to your real estate immediately, and ask them to repair or fix it yourself if you have a license.
Have at least one, or more fire extinguisher, and a fire blanket in your property for a fire emergency. Buy one fire

extinguisher for each of your cars as well. You can buy them as cheap as twenty dollars.

18-   Warning:

If you don't have an electrician certificate, never touch electricity. If you take this risk you may:
- Kill yourself
- Make fire
- Receive huge fines, or end up in jail

19-   Private medical insurance

In addition to basic governmental medical cover which exists in some countries, you can buy private insurance for your family, which is including more medical cover plus private hospital cover. They may include ambulance services as well.

Some example in Australia is as below:
- Medibank
- Bupa
- Etc.

Some of these companies even sign a contract with you without locking the duration of the contract. But, all of them have some waiting periods for some of their primary medical services.

In America and Canada, some employers provide private medical insurance to their employees in the remuneration package.

20-   Phone and Internet

In most third world countries, you pay at the end of the month as per your usage. In the developed countries, you can buy a plan, including a service package with a monthly payment for your home phone, mobile phone, and internet services. Some service providers in Australia are as below:

- Telstra
- Vodafone
- TPG
- Optus
- Etc.

Make sure you check all deals, and their network specifications before signing your contract.

21-   Pet

Having a pet in developed countries is very popular, including:

- Dog
- Cat

- Bird
- Guinea pig
- Mouse
- Snake
- Rabbit
- Etc.

Dogs are the most popular pet as they are very loyal and making a very close two-way relationship with families. Cats are the second popular one after the dogs.

I recommend you to buy proper medical insurance for your pet, as the cost of vet and emergency surgeries will not be affordable for many families.

I have a Japanese Spitz dog, and I enjoy having him. He is very kind and energetic and is making excellent connections with all members of the family.

In some cases, pets can help to treat or improve so many different sicknesses, especially mental issues like autism, depression, anxiety, etc.

Some pets, like dogs, need to go walking at least once a day. Make sure also you pick up your dog's poo from the street. Otherwise, you will ruin the face of your city, together with the risk of getting penalties.

You need to register your pets like cats and dogs with your local council and pay the fee. You can inject a traceability microchip under their skin by your vet to ensure you can find them once they get lost.

You must keep their immunization up-to-date as well. But it's not very expensive.

Dogs are brilliant. They can learn, on average up to 160 words. But, you should consider that an adult dog is like a three-year-old child. So, don't expect too much from them. Their passion, kindness, and attitude are better than some humans instead—lovely personality.

You can buy or adopt dogs and cats—particular organizations managing adoptions like "RSPCA" in Australia.

You can desex dogs, cats, and rabbits to avoid making children. In the case of a council registration fee, the desexed pet will be cheaper to pay. You should desex your pet at an early age.

22-   Other insurances

In addition to medical insurance, you can buy the following coverages for yourself, and your family to make your life risk-free as much as possible:

- Life insurance- For death, and permanent disability
- Home insurance- It's a must If you are the homeowner
- Home content insurance- For fire, theft, etc.
- Car insurance
- Unemployment insurance
- Business insurances

For car insurance in some countries, when you pay your annual registration, for example, $800, you are also covered for third-part accidental death. But, you need to buy even third-party damage insurance, and it's perfect also to obtain comprehensive coverage for your car to cover the cost of any accidental repair on your vehicle.

When you want to buy any insurance, you need to shop around, get quotes from a couple of companies, find the best price, bargain, and make a good deal.

Having multiple policies with one insurance company will give you discount benefits.

Some popular insurance companies in Australia are as below:
- RACV
- Allianz

- AAMI
- Some Banks
- Coles
- Etc.

23- Superannuation

In some developed countries like Australia, when you work, your employer, also, must pay an amount equivalent of nine to twelve percent of your salary to your superannuation account. This account is under government rule, and it's your saving for your retirement.

The companies managing these funds invest your money in many different industries like the stock market, construction, and real estate to increase your saving by making interest.

You are not allowed to use this money before your retirement except for some unusual circumstances. For example, during the Covid-19 crisis, people who were affected by the Covid-19 could withdraw up to $20000 of superannuation.

You can also register for a self-managed super fund. In this case, you will manage your superannuation fund.

24-   Investment

You have many different options for investing as per below:

- Real estate
- Stock market
- Bonds
- Gold and Silver
- Buy a business
- Buying or mining the cryptocurrency
- Write a book and earn royalties
- Make an invention, patent it, and earn royalties and licensing fee
- Buy collectibles like arts and antique cars, and keep them for appreciation
- Lend your money to people to gain interest
- Etc.

I know many people working in salary based jobs but invested in real estate. Following is some example for you to get a feeling about these options:

- A family moved to Australia 25 years ago- Have eight investment properties
- An Engineer has got three investment properties

- A scientist has got two investment properties

You can invest in something like the below list:
- Buy a vending machine and manage it
- Buy a small supermarket
- Buy a hedge fund
- Buy an index fund
- Buy a mutual fund
- Buy Bond
- Buy small properties
- Buy a property in a regional area
- Buy property in small cities other than your capital city
- Buy a car and rent it to a driver
- Buy a cafe and manage it
- Buy a company

I have a broker friend. He studied accounting and created a partnership with three of his classmates. They invest together and buy many properties. They earn the rent plus capital growth because of the appreciation of properties.

I'm not a fan of investing in lottery tickets and jackpot. But, so many people buy a ticket every week and hope one day they will become a millionaire.

25-   Credit card

The best money gurus recommend not to use credit cards, and loan at all. But, I would suggest using if:

- You can use that money to invest in a higher interest rate return
- You have to take it to buy your living necessary stuff, and you don't have any other options

If you have a job, it's straightforward to get credit cards and loans. But, also, it's effortless to fall in the credit cards trap. You spend, and you pay interest for un-necessary shopping. Actually, with credit cards and loans, your money makes other people productive. So, pay-off debts, and save money to buy in cash and invest with your savings. This approach is the only way to get rich and achieve financial freedom.

One significant opportunity around credit cards is "Balance transfer." You can transfer your debt on a credit card from one bank to another bank, and gain some benefits like having twelve months interest-free payment. You can do this more than one time.

26-   Safety

In developed countries, safety is essential. You need to consider safety everywhere, while driving, at work, at home, etc. Make sure you understand the requirement of safety in your area, especially in your workplace, and use proper PPE- Personal Protective Equipment- and never bridge the rules of safety. Otherwise, you will end up with some disastrous situation or being in jail.

27-   Security

The subject of security is vast and controversial. Back in Iran, we had to make a steel guard for all windows of our house. A window without guard was a very high risk for our home security.

In countries like Canada and Australia, none of the houses have window guards. In our neighborhood, people leave their bikes outside their home.

A teenager can walk alone in the street without any problem even at night. This situation is not safe in many countries. In general, I feel very relaxed living here when I see minimal crime. But, you still have to lock your doors and windows.

The scenario in America is different. I'm not convinced with any reasoning people and government of the United States bring for having a gun. One day, I asked an American scientist about guns. He said we keep guns to protect our family against criminals. Then I asked him what about your kids when they go to school by walk without you. Who protects them?

I believe gun accessibility for the public, even to people with mental sickness, is just adding insecurity and crime to society.

Anyway, these days also you can install remote control security cameras around your house and monitor your property through your smartphone.

28-   Loan

You have so many loan options, like:
- Home loan
- Car loan
- Personal loan
- Consolidation loan
- Business loan
- Peer-to-peer loan
- Etc.

As I mentioned before, take a loan only if you have to. Otherwise, you are losing money. It's better to save money and buy without paying interest.

Get broker's help for loans, as they are experts, and can find the best deals for you. Google everything to gather initial information for any of your loan, and purchase, before you act.

29-   Politics

While I believe that the version of democracy in none of the countries in the world is still perfect, but most developed countries have some level of democracy much better than developing and third world countries.

You will be participating in elections like below:
- Presidential election
- Parliamentary election
- Council election

Also, you may need to provide information for the national Census. Search and find out if these collaborations are mandatory or not. In some countries, your vote is compulsory and will get fine if you skip it.

30-   Helping others

If you are the kind of person who likes to help others, you have so many options—no need to pay beggars.

You can consider the following options:
- Work voluntary jobs
- Pay supportive organizations like "SALVOS," they support people in need
- Pay donations in reliable channels
- Lend your money to people in need like "Kiva.org."
- Support Science, reasoning, and secular values like" CFI- Center For Inquiry."

Or, search in your network and friends to find out if they know a family needing your help.

31-   Sport

You have so many options to start any game. You can choose and simply enroll in a class, and learn it. The limitation is as below:
- Your mind
- Your body
- Your budget
- The Climate

32-   Marriage

The culture and approach to marriage, to some extent, is much better in developed countries compared to traditional countries. In non-developed countries, many people still marry in conventional ways.

Sometimes, their parents choose their partner for them. In religious countries, having a relationship with the opposite gender is a crime. How can you find your lifetime partner without having a relationship with that person before marriage?

Fortunately, here you can be with your partner for any time you like before you decide about marriage.

Many third-world country's couples end up with divorce after they moved to developed countries and noticed they are not a perfect match for each other.

33-   Sex workers

Unfortunately, we can see a lot of crimes, family issues, insecurities, diseases, and other social disasters in the field of sex in so many countries. But, it's not the case in developed countries.

In developed countries, the sex worker is usually a legal and registered job with governmental support. They eliminated all adverse effects of non-developed country's approaches to this field.

34-   Will

If you would like to make a safe and secure future for your kids in case of your and your wife's accidental death, you can prepare a particular document called "will" by the help of a lawyer. You need to pay a couple of hundred dollars to make and record your will in the lawyer's office.

In the will document, you can nominate your kids or your spouse to receive all or part of your assets, and capital after you die. If you don't prepare a will, the process for your spouse or your kids to receive the benefits after you die will be much longer, and a little troublesome.

35-   Car accident

In case of a car accident, you should pull over your car in a safe place if possible. Then meet with other car's driver, and hand over the detail of you, your address, contact number, and both car detail. Then you call your insurance company and explain the accident. They will judge based on the scenario and will act as per your insurance policy. Make sure you take plenty of pictures from your damaged car, other cars, and the scene of the accident. You will need to provide them with your insurance company.

If you are at fault, you have to pay the excess amount, which is zero to something like $700 depends on your car value and your insurance policy detail.

If the accident damaged a third-party property, for example, a third car, or the wall of a house, or someone got hurt, you have to call the ambulance and police to manage the scene and finalize the situation for you.

If the car is not repairable, they will write – off your vehicle and will pay the lump-sum of the car value to you.

36-   Funeral

Very different from some other countries, which people hold funerals in religious venues. Here usually, people use unique funeral houses for this purpose. But, also some people hold it in the church as well.

You can pay the funeral cost by installment, or sometimes you have this cost covered from your life insurance depends on your policy.

37-   Police

In many countries, the police force is visible everywhere in the city, but people bribe them quickly and skip the rules.

In developed countries, you rarely see the police force in the streets, but in case of crime, they will be present very quickly, and their performance is high. You can not survive with bribing police force in these countries.

The police force is very friendly and sophisticated.

38-   Selling property

To sell a house, you need to talk to a real estate. They will prepare professional pictures and will advertise your property. You have to pay a specific commission after they sold your property. Selling a property without support from real estate is possible, but it is not easy.

39-   Selling car

You can prepare proper pictures after cleaning and washing your car. Then you have to list it on a car sale websites. Some of these websites are free, and some of them charge you about $60. People will contact you and ask for a discount, but finally, the price depends on the value of your car and your urgency.

40-   Waste management

In developed countries, you must separate your wastes in different categories, including at least three groups of "Recycle," "General waste," and "Garden waste."
    In some countries like Sweden, you must separate them in more than three categories. We also have the local council's support to collect the hard wastes like:

- Old TV
- Old furniture
- The building, and renovation wastes
- Etc.

Each council has a different system and schedule for collecting hard wastes.

You must keep special and hazardous wastes separately, and you must deliver them to the council's waste management centers. For example:

- Batteries
- Paint
- Chemical
- Lamps
- Etc.

41- DIY and BYO

DIY stands for Do-It-Yourself and means you buy materials, and make the stuff yourself for your purpose. For example, in Australia, the stores of "Bunnings" sells a lot of things which you can do DIY.

BYO stands for Bring-Your-Own and is used in some restaurants basically to show that they don't serve alcoholic drinks, but you can bring your alcohol, and drink it with your meal in this restaurant.

42- Events

We have many events every year, to mention some of the international affairs the list is as below:

- Christmas
- Halloween
- Easter

- Labor day
- Mother's day
- New year eve

There are also many special events for each country, like:
- Movember
- Harmony day
- Anzac day
- Etc.

43-   Bargain

Usually, the business model in developed countries is a no-bargain business model. But, be aware that this is for small purchases like clothing, foods, shoes, etc.

To buy a property, a car, etc., you must bargain to get a better price.

In some countries like China, you can use a bargain even to buy cheaper things like foods or shoes.

44-   Citizenship

Usually, each developed country has its process for citizenship. In some states, you must stay, for example, four years as a permanent resident, and then apply for citizenship. Then you will pass a test regarding your knowledge about history, and the political system of the country, and sometimes a language test. If you pass all these, you will receive your citizenship certificate in a special ceremony.

45-   Tax return

Once a year after the end of June, you have to sit with your accountant or a tax return expert and report your annual income, then the system will calculate if you paid the correct amount of tax or not. In some cases, you entitle with some money to return to you, as you had some work-related expenses, and you paid more than required.

You can keep all work-related receipts, and claim in the tax return session. These claims can be following items as an example:

- Computer and Laptop
- Phone
- Internet
- Uniform
- Work shoes
- Petrol
- Office furniture
- Etc.

46-   Aged care

Very different from non-developed countries, which people keep their old parents at home, in developed countries, almost 95% of couples work, and none of them can stay home and care for the elderly parents. So after their ability to self-care, and self-manage reach to the edge, people, enroll their parents in an Aged care facility, or a nursing home.

In nursing homes, they have full support, including initial needs and medical supports. If a family can't afford the cost of aged care, the government will cover the cost.

47-   Home movement

In case of moving your stuff from one to another rental home, or when you buy your own home, you have the following options:

- Transfer your material with your car
- Transfer your stuff with a rental van or a rental truck, but you drive
- Hire a vehicle with the removal team, and they transfer everything for you

48- Discount systems

You enroll for a discount system, and they send you the card like "Flybuys" for Coles supermarket, or "Everyday rewards card" for Woolworth supermarket. Then, whenever you purchase in their supermarket, you scan your card. Each purchase gives you some positive points depends on the value of your purchase. After a while, you and your partner collect a couple of thousands of credit points. At that time you can use your points to get a discount on your future purchases, or you can buy some goods for free.

This system is the case for many retail stores as well, but they register you as a member, and you will get a discount if you shop in their store frequently.

49- Sales

Many people love sales. Especially, ladies are the bigger fan of shopping and sales events. In developed countries, each store decides to put some goods on sales condition based on many different reasons like the following:

- To empty a shelf from last items of a batch

- To sell the products which expire soon
- To encourage customers to come to their shop
- To make a habit of shopping from them frequently
- To support long term benefits

One thing to tell you, don't be too excited when you see sales, because it is an ongoing event in these markets. Only some special days of sales are occasions—for example, the "Boxing day," which is the day after charismas day. On this day, most stores put many items for selling at lower prices, and they sell a high quantity of products.

Also, you can be a smart shopper, if you buy on sales grocery and supermarket items every time you go shopping. But, make sure only to buy whatever you consume.

50- Selling stuff

If you don't need some good thing, you can convert them to cash quickly. For example, in Australia, you have these options:
- Cash convertor stores
- Gumtree.com.au
- Other convertor stores

Some people also place their stuff in front of their house and note them as "For free," then people can pick them up if they need them. Don't put usable materials in landfills. We have only one planet to live at the moment.

Chapter 6
Shocks

As you may expect, moving to a new country will have some surprises for anyone, and this comes from differences, which is not a bad thing, but sometimes it will make trouble for you. The main wonders, and sometimes shocks are as below:

1- Language shock

You can't understand their language even if you thought you learned that language already. This situation can happen because:

a- You don't know their accent
b- You don't know the usage of some words
c- Some native people don't consider you are immigrant and

you don't have their language skill
level

This problem happened to me once I arrived in Melbourne. When I paid the taxi driver, he asked me if I have "change." I had no idea about "change" while I knew the meaning of this word. Finally, my friend came to my help and said he is asking for coins.

The second day, I went to a real estate to search for rental property. Despite having an IELTS certificate, which is an international English test system, I was not able to understand even one word when the girl explained something to me. It took many months to me until I improve a little, and it took me a couple of years to get back to my language confidence level.

After nine years, I'm still learning English, and I'm sure it will not end in my whole life.

One good recommendation is to join a "Toastmaster" club. They gather fortnightly and chat about everything in a structured manner. Toastmaster can improve your language and social skills, together with expanding your network.

You can also learn the local language by reading unique books, like:

- Canadian English
- American English
- Australian English
- Understanding everyday Australian- three books
- Slang dictionaries
- Etc.

Learning slangs is very useful for understanding local people, but be careful not to use them unless you are 100% sure about the context and meaning. Using slang in the wrong situation can mean disastrous. I recommend you focus on the primary language first and learn slang after that.

2- Cultural shock

Any country has a different culture, and some of them are special as below:

- Polite culture
- Rude culture
- Frank culture
- Having a sense of humor
- Respect too much
- Hiding their actual message
- Using too much body language

- Not using body language
- Touching the audience while speaking
- Asking personal questions
- Following the rules and laws
- Not caring about the rules

It's your talent that comes to your help. You need to watch and understand the culture first, because people maybe don't mean to annoy you, but you are annoyed, or they possibly want to be very friendly, but you feel offended.

For me, it was not a shock, because I have visited many countries before my immigration, but it was a happy surprise when I noticed people are very polite.

Here is Australia, people consider city cleanliness, they are very polite, and they help each other a lot. But, for sure, good and bad people live in every country. It's mostly their governmental system and their laws and rules that determine how ordinary people behave. For example, stringent regulations and expensive penalties make people drive correctly. In contrast, in some countries un-effective penalty system or ability to bribe the police force causes ordinary people to drive like crazy.

Make sure you don't stay home even if you don't have a job. Go out for following activities in addition to time that you put for job search:

- Shopping
- Festivals
- Local events
- Exhibitions
- Parties
- Community gathering and activities
- Your religion activities and gathering
- Go to the park and talk to local people

This way, you can expand your familiarity with local culture, and expand your network together with refreshing your mind and avoiding depression.

One of the surprises for some immigrants, especially for traditional families, and cultures, is the relation between girls and boys. Here, girls and boys have a very open and relaxed relationship, and they can go to each other's homes.

I'm an advocate of this culture because this is a real need for teenagers. But, for many people, this is a challenge against their religion. You can teach your kids to follow your culture, but be careful, sometimes kids won't accept your mindset, and they will judge, and choose whatever they think is better, and correct.

3- Price shock

If you are moving from a third-world country to a developed country, be ready to see a massive jump in your living cost. In some cases, the price of a bottle of water can be more than ten times.

If you spend your savings, and your saving is from your home country, its bad news, you will run out of money. So, don't wait to find the best job. Start working whatever you can do but search for your career.

Once you got a job, you will be safe, as the inflation is meager, in some cases near to zero.

Don't forget, working the only husband, or the single wife won't be the right solution in developed countries, because if one person works:

- It's tough to cover the living cost of family
- It's almost impossible to buy a house

- It's very dull for staying at home, and you will be depressed

The good news is that in developed countries, the price of goods is almost constant. The cost of bread, for example, today is very similar to its price ten years ago.

The rental price of properties has a raise of about two to three percent per year and its negotiable. If you think that the rental increase is not fair, you can complain to the related government department.

Another good news for single parents is that the government provides special supports to single parents as well.

4- Technology surprise

In developed countries, you will use technologies everywhere. Your life is much easier as per below:

- You can buy almost everything online
- You can find anything on the Internet
- You can reach any solution and any new products available in the world

So, be ready to be flexible, and learn new things every day. For example, you can pay all of your bills online by using Bpay. Or you can book a hotel, a cruise trip, a cinema, and almost everything through their website.

I remember, twenty years ago, we went to Dubai for an automotive industry exhibition, and after visiting the show, we visited the Jumeirah beach. On the way back to the hotel, we waited more than five minutes in front of the beach in the street for the traffic light to become green. Surprisingly, there was not any car there, but our traffic light was still red.

Finally, my colleague noticed there is a push-button on the base of the traffic light, and he guessed maybe we should push it. Yes, that was the answer to activate the timer.

This sort of technology needs your flexibility and sense of discovery and investigation. But it's okay because it's making your life easier and safer.

Here is some more example that you will see, and learn very quickly but some of them still doesn't exist in third-world countries:

- The self-check-out machine in supermarkets
- Push button for the traffic light
- Automatic highway toll payment
- Park meter
- Vending machines

Chapter 7
Deep Dive

In this chapter, I will help you with the job-hunting process, business solutions, and related challenges.

A- Deep dive

I had very high professional positions back home in my country. When I moved, I had one year looking for a suitable job.

Let's go to detail to understand the situation better as this can happen to most people except some lucky people who also have exceptional skills.

My highest position in Iran was" Vice president" of a company with 150+ personnel. My salary was very high compared to the average wage at the time. I moved to Australia, and in the first two weeks, I applied for 30 jobs related to my profession, and my experience. Not even one call from employers. So disappointed, continued to search and apply.

The first three months passed quickly. I enrolled in a course for resume writing and job hunting. At the end of the course, I started a practical placement in a sheet metal manufacturing company. After completing the placement period, they didn't offer me any job.

Six months passed, and I was paying rent, and I also bought a car. The cost of the kinder garden for my son also added. My wife was attending an English class for six months, and then six months in an Aged Care training course.

I summarize the story, one year passed, and I ran out of money. During the one year which I was applying for my professional jobs, I tried some casual jobs to make some cash, including:

- Newspaper distribution
- Painting of buildings
- Carpentry workshop
- Pizza delivery

None of them made more than 20% of my family's living costs, and I was using my savings. After one year, finally, I got a job—a "Production supervisor" position with a reasonably good salary.

You see. I dived deeply from a very high position in my home country to a very lower casual place in a new country. Finally, the first professional position also was very much lower than my capabilities and my achievements back home.

This scenario is a typical scenario for many people while immigrating. But, you should be positive and not giving up until you achieve your goals. Later in this chapter, I will share many scenarios that people with skilled or business visas or refuge visas came to a new country, and built their future. You will be able to compare your situation with some of the real case scenarios and make your plan based on your findings.

B- Skilled jobs

If you are coming with a skilled visa, or you are a refugee, but you have a skill, you have an excellent chance to find a job in your field. But, this may take time in some cases and may happen very quickly in some other cases.

Here is some example:

- A young Civil Engineer applied online for a job from overseas and received sponsorship from an employer in the field of dam construction. Then he received a sponsorship visa and traveled to Australia. He started his work immediately after arrival. This excellent achievement can happen if your skill or degree is very on-demand in the target market.

- I came here with a Bachelor's and a Master's Degree in Mechanical Engineering and fourteen years of experience. It took one year to get my first professional job. I have done pizza delivery with a casual agreement and a meager wage for six months. But, during the pizza job, I got two interviews with the connection provided via pizza shop customers. I was chatting with customers whenever it was possible, and some people, especially people with my nationality, was trying to help me. Finally, one of these connections interviews ended my journey to my first professional job. Isn't it exciting?

- I started with the Production supervisor role with two sections only. I got then promotion to the same position for six departments. Two years after that, I got promoted to Production manager and project manager roles. Recently, I'm applying for Operations manager roles and General manager roles, which are the roles that I had in my home country before my immigration.

- A friend of mine, a Senior Electrical Engineer, attended in the course of job hunting and participated in a practical placement in a custom-design-machinery manufacturer. He ended up with a job offer and started with the same company. His salary was minimal but still was an excellent point to start as a professional position.

- Another Electrical Engineer with skill, and experience of SCADA, spent seven months and found the first job in another state. When he moved with his family to that city, they didn't like the town, and he resigned. It took another three months for him to find his next job.

- An IT engineer with very new and high-level programming skills found her job just before the ending of the first month after arrival.
- A friend of mine with Mechanical Engineering degree, and fourteen years of experience in automotive industries, worked two and a half years in carpentry as a process worker until he found a Design Engineer position in an automotive manufacturing company.
- A Civil Engineer accepted a job in a tiny regional city and stayed with his family for about two years to make a local experience. Then found a better position in the capital city as a senior engineer.
- A friend of mine, with a Civil Engineering degree and many years of project executive experience, was not able to find a professional job even after three years. He worked in carpentry for three years, then attended a training course for tiling, and started working for a tiling company.

- An IT Engineer had a couple of contract roles in his field but was not able to find a permanent job in his profession. Finally, disappointed with his degree, and started his own carpentry business. He mostly used google and searched the internet for many different design guides for building wooden structures, and was able to survive with his own business.
- A Chemistry PhD was not able to find a position in his field but established business for web-design.
- An educated couple came with a student visa and studied PhD in Australia. One of them secured a teaching position in a university, and her partner found an Engineering job.
- A Bachelor of Forestry, without any work experience, came to Australia. She learned English in six months and attended an Aged Care training course for the second six months and was able to secure a permanent job in an aged care facility.
- A friend of mine with a Child care degree came to Australia and did a course of child care here, and after

receiving her certificate, secured a position in a child care facility.

- An expert in tailoring, started with working for a tailor shop for only $7 an hour while the minimum legal wage was $18 an hour. After one year, she used her payslip together with her husband to apply for a home loan. After buying their home, she did a child care course but was not able to find a job. Finally, a friend introduced her to an aged care facility, and she got a role in the kitchen of aged care.
- A pharmacy experienced person came to Australia and persisted in finding her professional job. She didn't do any university studies here. After four years, she is still without any position.
- A Chemical Engineer came with work and holiday one year visa to Australia, and she applied for a position in a medical instrument manufacturing company. She was able to secure a sponsored visa from that company and worked with that employer.
- A Mechanical Engineer lady with experience in the automotive industry got a job only after a couple of months

in an automotive parts manufacturing company.

- A young student completed his study in accounting in Australia and got a job in a big bank. Five years after that, he gained promotion to a senior lending manager role.
- A friend of mine studied a Master's degree in Mechanical Engineering in Malaysia, then studied PhD in Australia, and now is working in an engineering company.
- A Mechanical Engineer with a Master's degree moved to Canada, started with a casual role as a QC inspector, and still searching for a higher position.
- An Engineer moved to Canada, and never searched for engineering jobs. He did a plumber training course and started his own plumbing business immediately.
- A Master's degree in Electrical Engineer moved to Canada, was not able to find his job. After one year working in cabinet making, he studied another Master's degree in Canada, then found an Engineering job.

- A Bachelor of IT without professional experience settled in a process worker job in a medical instrument manufacturing company.
- A Polymer Engineer was not able to find an engineering job in Australia. But, with his skills in CNC machining, he is already working four years as a CNC programmer and operator.
- A refugee came to Australia by boat, started as mechanic worked for someone a couple of years. Then he established his own excavating business.
- A refugee came by boat to Australia, has mechanic skills, bought a van, and started a mobile mechanic business.
- A Muslim Engineer attended a church and asked them for help. They helped him to find a job.
- A medical doctor moved to Canada and gave up her profession.
- A medical doctor moved to Australia and did relevant courses and studies, was able to validate her degree, and started working on her real profession.

- A Mechanical Engineer started his first job as a salesperson of HVAC systems six months after his arrival.

Now you have a better feeling and understanding about many different possible scenarios that can happen to anyone depends on their situation, their skills, and the time. I now will explain a structured approach to what to do to be successful in your career once you arrived:

1- Make a professional resume and cover letter

For resume, and cover letter writing, if you are not a native language, don't waste your time writing it yourself. You must find a professional native resume writer and pay to prepare a professional document.

I revised my resume myself so many times without any positive feedback. Finally, when I paid $800 for my resume and cover letter to an expert, my resume started getting feedback.

Be aware that, usually, employers ask for two referees. These should be people who worked with you before—for example, your former manager, or your former colleague. If you don't have anyone, use your friends as a referee, but if they are professionals in their field, they can introduce you in a better way.

After they interviewed you, and they were happy with the interview, they will call your referees, and ask many questions to discover your strength, weaknesses, and your attitude. They will make the final decision about hiring you only after speaking with your referees.

In sporadic cases, like the one I had recently, the employer skips the referee call if they are so confident about your performance, and your attitude.

You need to inform your referees about the employer's call.

2- Enroll in employment, resume writing or job hunting courses

I noticed every country has this kind of course. In Australia, they call it "ESL Employment." You can do it in a "Tafe" center.

3- Do a placement

You can find a placement after you did the ESL course. Also, you can search and find a good company related to your profession and communicate with them. Ask them to let you work for three months for free. At the end of three months, if you are right, and they need you, they will hire you. If not, at least, you made a three months local experience.

4- Do voluntary work

You can find any kind of voluntary work in any field that you can. In this way, you will improve your language, you will make a network of people, and you will become familiar with the new culture.

5- Do casual jobs

At the same time that you are searching for your job, search, and find some casual jobs. In this way, you make money, you will spend fewer savings, you will make a network, and you will improve your cultural awareness and your language.

6- Expand your network as much as possible by attending local events, professional events, conferences, festivals, etc.

7- Enroll for professional courses

Search and find out what professional skills are essential in the market of your profession, and you don't have them. Invest in yourself by enrolling in the courses and learn them. Add it to your resume, and empower your capabilities and your chance.

8- Continue studying language

Never stop your language study and improvement.

9- Attend professional shows and exhibitions

There will be so many shows and exhibitions in every industry. You can upgrade your information about your industry and market by visiting them.

10- Create your LinkedIn page

The best and the most popular professional social network in the world is LinkedIn. Create an account, and add your page if you still don't have one.

In a developed country, many recruiters and employers search on LinkedIn to find their required talents. Make sure your page is professional. For example:

- Add a professional picture with a smile
- Add all of your experiences and skills
- Add all of your related certificates

- Use the content of your professionally written resume to complete your LinkedIn page instead of writing it yourself if your language is not native
- Keep your page up-to-date
- Add your friends and network to your connections
- Add some professional people from LinkedIn to your connections even if you don't know them
- Share professional posts frequently. In this way, people in your connection will see you often, and if they are recruiters, or they are looking for talents, they will review your profile
- Endorse your friends and your connections for their skills. In this way, they will endorse you as well
- Write a recommendation for your friends, and colleagues, and ask them to write one for you
- Check LinkedIn's job page frequently, and apply for suitable positions
- Join related LinkedIn groups, and follow their posts
- Upgrade to LinkedIn premium if you can afford it. It's $40 per months and gives you more insight

11- Find out what are the popular job search websites

For example, in Australia, the most popular sites are "Seek" and "Indeed."

12- Check the job hunting websites, and find out which positions you can apply

13- If you can apply for different positions, you may need to prepare different resumes for each of them.

14- If the different positions you can apply are in the same field and category, you may not need to have more than one resume, which is much easier

15- Check every day for new job ads, and apply for suitable jobs

16- Keep your mobile phone with you all the time. Each call can be an interview

17- If you received a call, and you can't talk at that moment or that place, apologize and ask their agreement for you to call them back in a short time after that in a good situation, and a proper position.

18- Don't be anxious and stressed when you receive a call. Speak calmly, and answer clearly with confidence. The first call is the initial assessment of your skill, language, attitude, and communication quality.

19- Some employers hire directly, and some others ask a recruiter company to interview and hire for them

20- If they invited you for an interview, dress professionally, preferably, suit and tie.

21- For some positions, wearing a suit and tie is not a positive point, for example, for a hands-on production supervisor role.

22- Check their website, and gather information about their company before your interview

23- List down some points as usually the interviewers ask you if you have any questions at the end of their interview.

24- If they ask you what your expected salary is, the best answer is that my salary is negotiable. What is your range of pay for this role? Then if their answer satisfied you, you accept, and if it's not reasonable, mention your expectations.

25- For the first job, accept any salary. Lower your expectation. You can search and find a better job after that. You need a local experience ASAP.

26- Usually, all employers consider a three or six months probationary period, and your contract will be extended after that only if they are happy with your work and attitude.

27- When you started a new job, don't rush to show yourself. Spend sufficient time to become familiar with the system, people, work culture, and their values. Keep your improvement ideas for a suitable time.

28- Match your behavior with the culture of the company if you see they have a good one. If they need a culture change, don't hurry. Take your time. Sometimes, if you act too much in your probationary period, they will miss-understand you, or some nasty people will report against you and will ruin your chance of success and stay.

29- Consider Continuous Improvement in any role

Note: This following information is handy for you as you are new in the workplace:

30- Workplace culture: The workplace culture will be different in each country. For example, In America, they usually work hard and under pressure. They stay for overtime a lot. Work is a priority. But, in Australia, you will see the workplace is more relaxed than in America. People behave more informally, and most of them think about work-life balance.

31- Discrimination, Racism, and Harassment, especially sexual harassment, is a severe crime. The first thing you will notice is that you receive an employer handbook, and they explain these crucial matters in it.

32- You will learn about disciplinary actions in the workplace. If someone skipped the rules, or has low performance, or bypass the safety rules, and issues like these, management team or human resource department will run disciplinary action for that person. The disciplinary actions can be in the following steps:

- Counseling session
- Verbal warning- recorded
- Written warning
- Termination of job

33- You usually will have twenty-five days of annual leave, ten days of sick leave, three days of carer's leave, and two days of compassionate leave per one year of work. You will have three months long service leave after ten years of service. You will have to participate in Jury duty role in court randomly when the government asks you to do. These will change country to country.

34- Performance appraisal is the review and evaluation of your performance and regularly implemented, every six months, or in some companies every year. The results can be as follow:

- Pay rise
- Promotion
- Warning
- Termination
- Development plan
- Etc.

35- The phone is not allowed in some companies. If you are a process worker, you can't use it in any company.

36- Vision, mission, and values of each business is vital. You should try to find out and understand it before it's too late.

37- Each business has an organization chart. Of course, many of them don't have one. But, the positions from top to down can be like this but different in any company:

- Chairman
- Board of directors
- CEO

- Managing director
- General manager
- Operations manager
- Factory manager
- Production manager, Sales, and Marketing Manager, Engineering and R&D manager, QC and QA manager, IT manager, HR manager, Finance manager
- Assistant production manager
- OH&S representative
- Sales agent
- Team leader
- Line leader, Leading hand
- Process worker

38- HR or human resource department is a very considerable authority in developed countries. The power of the HR manager is much higher than even an Operations manager.

39- When you started working in a new company, find out what is the KPI- Key performance indicators- of your department, and what is your role's KPI, if there is any. You will be assessed based on your KPI.

40- Consider that usually in America, Canada, Australia, and some similar countries, people calling each other's first names when they call each other in the workplace. This behavior is against the culture of many other countries, which they call each other by using the title, and surname, which is very formal and challenging.

Hopefully, you have talent and skills, and you will be successful.

C- Casual jobs

There are plenty of opportunities to start some casual jobs. I have already explained the benefits of informal employment as temporary solutions for professionals.

It's also a solution for people without special skills. But, after getting a casual job, always look for a permanent position, which is much better as job security and payment for superannuation and retirement.

You should search in your new country, and find out if there is a website or app for casual jobs as well. For example, in Australia, you can find some jobs in "au.jura.com" as well. This website can help you if you don't have skills either.

Another example is the app "Air tasker," you can search and find non-regular and some regular casual jobs in this app. I know an engineer who moved to Australia and was not able to find his professional position. He survived with Airtasker by doing Furniture assembly jobs he was getting every week in this app. The air tasker is active in the UK and Australia.

Generally, you will see two types of casual jobs:
- Legal casual job
- Illegal casual job

In legal casual jobs, you sign a contract, you pay tax, and the employer pays superannuation for you, but the employer doesn't have a commitment for your contract period. They can ask you any day to not come to work from tomorrow.

In illegal casual jobs, the employer pays you less than minimum legal payment, you don't pay tax, they don't pay your superannuation, and they pay you in cash. The employer doesn't have any commitment to your working future, either.

Some employers underpay their workers to avoid paying tax and superannuation. Unfortunately, many people have to accept this condition because they don't have better options.

Some example of casual jobs:
- Waiter and Waitress
- Driver
- Pizza shop and pizza delivery
- Painting for buildings
- Newspaper and brochure distribution
- Process worker
- Retail worker
- Hairdresser
- Etc.

Students usually have to do casual jobs. They can do all different positions as per availability, demand, and working limit of their visa.

Teenagers can work legally after the age of 15 in some countries, and younger than that is illegal. The culture of teenagers working is very healthy and useful for their future.

D- Businesses

Here are some scenario examples of people immigrated with business visa:

- A businessman came to Australia and established a particular language radio channel for his nationality.
- An automotive parts manufacturer came to Australia, and bought a pizza shop, and managed the shop with help from his wife, and his sons.
- A business owner with a company in the electrical industry moved to Canada and established a similar engineering company in Canada.
- An Engineer moved to Canada but purchased a supermarket, and personally worked in the store.
- Two partners came with a business visa, purchased a café for $280000, and had to sell it for $80000 after two years because the business and its location was not profitable enough.

- A refugee bought a pizza shop for $30000 because the council had a plan already to demolish that area by two years. He managed his shop for two profitable years.
- A refugee started a kebab shop and established three more branches of his brand after a couple of years.
- Many people are starting a particular supermarket like Indian or Persian one, and import goods from their country for their shop, and sell to their people.
- There are many restaurants with specialties of one country like an Indian restaurant, and Persian restaurant. Many of them have a very profitable business, because many people miss their country foods, and buy their services frequently.
- A couple came to Australia 27 years ago. The lady had an HR degree and established a recruitment company.
- A man with a business visa opened his jewelry shop in Melbourne precisely the same as the one he had overseas. He frequently travels to Asian

countries, and import products for his shop.

- A businessman imports Persian branded goods and distributes it in all Persian supermarkets around the country.
- A refugee started a computer shop with his partner, who is an IT specialist, and they import computer parts from China with their own branded label and sell in their shop. They also provide troubleshooting services to companies around.

- A man with a skilled visa and MBA degree started a HALAL foods restaurant.
- A bank manager with an MBA degree bought a pizza shop and managed it profitably.
- Two engineers established an engineering company for 3D printing and prototyping.
- A PhD student invented a new product, and used crowdfunding platforms like "Kick starter," and "Indiegogo" to pre-sell his product, and started manufacturing of his brand.

- A young boy finished his high school, started his buy-upgrade-sell Laptop business from home.
- A refugee started her own food products manufacturing business from her home kitchen.
- A businessman makes accessories of kayaks in a shed in his backyard.
- An Engineer created a partnership with his brothers, and they buy old properties at a reasonable price, renovate, and resell them at a higher price.
- A chemical engineer started his sole trade gardening business.
- A refugee started his sole trade tiling business.
- A refugee started a franchise mobile dog washing business.
- An engineer started manufacturing some metallic parts for a pharmaceutical company in which he is working there as an employee.
- A refugee opened his mechanic shop.
- An agriculture engineer has his sole trade painting business.

- A businessman started his Currency Exchange company the same as the one he had in his home country.

There are many options in front of you for starting a business, including but not limited as below:

- Pay a business broker, and get consultant services to buy a profitable business
- Search in "business for sale" websites, and find out the deals
- Search for "businesses in liquidation stage," and find out the deals
- Search for franchise opportunities, and buy one
- Establish a business similar to what you have in your home country if there is a demand for it
- Start a home business like food manufacturing, or consultancy business
- Buy products from china, and sell in eBay or Amazon
- Make educational, or informative videos and upload in YouTube
- Make digital courses and sell online
- Establish RTO- Registered Training Organization

- Buy used stuff, upgrade or repair them, and resell them on online platforms like local market places
- Establish an online business and sell products
- Design new Apps
- Etc.

You can advertise in many ways:
- Local newspapers
- YouTube
- Social media like Instagram and Facebook
- TV and Radio channels
- Etc.

For most businesses, you need governmental permission. For example, for a home-based food business, you need at least council permission, and if it's dairy products, you need dairy safe organization's approval too.

Usually, there are many grants and funding available by the government for small businesses. Search, and find out what sort of funding is available in your country and if you are eligible for it.

E- Freelancer

Freelancing means you work from home as you have a skill or profession. For examples, you can do the following projects online as a freelancer:

- 3D Design
- 2D Design
- Business plan preparation
- Project management
- Book cover design
- Brochure design
- Book editing
- Accounting
- Web design
- Programming and coding
- Mechanical analysis
- Consultancy
- Lawyer services
- App design
- Etc.

There is not a limitation for freelancer jobs. You just need to search in freelancer websites and apps, and register as a service provider, then search for projects and give a quote. If project owners select you, you will do the job, and they pay to your account.

Some freelancer websites and apps are as below:

- Fiverr
- Upwork
- Toptal
- PeoplePerHour
- Nexxt
- TaskRabbit
- Aquent
- Writer Access
- Skyword
- Freelancer
- Guru

If you have a useful skill, you can rely on this job approach.

F- Trade work

A good example is the app "Service seeking." You can register as a trade person or contractor in this app and quote for related projects. If customer choose you, you can do the job and earn money. This app is active in Australia only, but there are similar apps in each country.

Chapter 8
Boost Your Growth

You read so far seven chapters and noticed you might encounter a deep dive in the start for your career in a new country, unless you are fortunate, or your skills are entirely valid and matched with the modern market.

Now that you noticed the challenges in front of you, your mind is ready to overcome all obstacles.

The good news is that you don't need to stop at some minimum level of your profession, because you think you are an immigrant. Some people believe the high positions are only for native citizens, but this is not true.

Some people think they have to stick to minimum achievement, as they are so conservative and don't take risks to grow.

In developed countries, although there are some racist behaviors from some close-minded people, most people are open-minded and educated and respect all humans.

Even people with racist mind-set are fully aware of the consequences of racist actions and behaviors. In the developed countries, race, skin color, and nationality are not very important, and the first criteria for being selected in a role is competency.

How much you will grow depends on how much effort you put to upgrade yourself, and what is the limit of your mind.

Upgrading includes:

- Your language skills
- Your professional skills
- Your attitude
- Your soft skills like communication skill
- Your Emotional Intelligence skills
- Being open-minded and flexible
- Your ability to work with teams
- Your ability to learn new things every day

So, you want to be an Intelligent Immigrant, which is the title of this book. Besides to be aware of all information which I provided in this book, and implementing them, also consider these recommendations, and apply them:

1- Start with smaller positions, and make the experience
2- Respect people
3- Work toward the business vision, mission, and company's goals
4- Grow with promotions, or move to higher positions when you learned enough from current job
5- Look for the unanswered problems
6- Find achievements enjoyable
7- Be confident, think big, think positive
8- Learn new skills related to your profession
9- Study higher degrees in the fields that you are passionate about
10- Expand your network
11- Be never satisfied with the current status and make continuous improvement mind-set
12- See the big picture, and think out of the box

13- Be open-minded, be informative, and open your eyes and ears to all information

14- Make a couple of goals step by step, and act toward them

15- Have a competitive attitude

16- Apply new knowledge in your work as soon as possible

The most beautiful saying which I've heard is from Mark Zuckerberg which famously said:

"The biggest risk is not taking any risk."

This saying means if you stay idle, and if you don't change anything, and hope that everything will be fine if you don't move, unfortunately, this is not true. One day, your employer sends you home with redundancy. One day your employer's quality will improve, and you won't be good enough to stay more. One day, your low-speed attitude will cost you a lot.

So, be optimistic, passionate, and learn every day. Improve yourself every day until one day you feel you achieved whatever you could obtain back in your home country.

"Sky is the limit."

I agree that achieving the same level of goals in your home country is much more comfortable, but you don't have a choice to do that. You have chosen to move and make a better living for yourself and your family.

So, do it 100%, not 50%.

Chapter 9
Final Word

I hope this book added motivation with some helpful knowledge to you, and you are satisfied with reading it and putting your time on it—congratulation on finishing another book.

I wrote this book the way that is applicable for any developed country, and I added some Australian specific examples as well.

"I wanted to hit two targets with one arrow."

I hope my effort was successful, and you are happy with my book.

I also started writing my next book, which is the "High Achievers."

The story in this book is about:
- How to choose suitable professions with the potential of massive growth

- How to achieve your full potential
- How to be more than ordinary people
- How to influence people around you
- How to impact your society and your world
- How to be more competitive

If you like to continue and learn, you can read this book too.